W. H. AUDEN

FRANCIS SCARFE

W. H. AUDEN

THE LYREBIRD PRESS
LITERARY EDITIONS : J. B. HANSON
THE RAMPARTS
MONACO
1949

I

IN 1891, in an interview with Jules Huret, Mallarmé is reported to have said : " Surtout manqua (à Hugo) cette notion indiscutable : que dans une société sans stabilité, sans unité, il ne peut se créer d'art stable, d'art définitif. De cette organisation sociale inachevée, qui explique en même temps l'inquiétude des esprits, naît l'inexpliqué besoin d'individualité dont les manifestations littéraires présentes sont le reflet direct. "

We are entitled to feel surprised at Mallarmé's brilliant intuition of the Marxist approach to literature, and his complete exposition, in a few words, of the central problem of the artist in contemporary society. Though more than fifty years have passed, the artist's position is unchanged. Neither Europe nor any part of it has achieved that social order and equilibrium from which a definitive art might emerge. ~~although there~~ *although there are*

F.S. ~~hopes and signs that our stability will be achieved in~~

Russia ~~Russia.~~ / *Inquiétude* is still the dominating feature in writers and writing today. The poet still wrestles with the temptation to individualism, and seeks in vain to integrate himself in an unintegrated social pattern. Like Mallarmé, he feels that he is condemned to " sculpt his own tomb ", though he now has the consolation that in " sculpting his own tomb " Mallarmé at least erected a beautiful and lasting monument to intelligence.

Few poets, since Mallarmé, have attempted to achieve a synthesis, though many, like Rilke, Eliot, Pound, Valéry, have striven to transcend the personal. We must agree, with Valéry, that it is unlikely that the twentieth century can reproduce the " universal man ". Of the few who have attempted the synthesis in poetry, one of the most outstanding in England has been W.H. Auden. It is perhaps not an exaggeration to say that, for his own generation, Auden has been something of a Hugo, attempting the impossible with very inadequate materials, and being obliged to make the most of his weaknesses.

Wystan Hugh Auden, born in York on February 21st 1907, had all the advantages and disadvantages of a bourgeois up-bringing. He was the son of highly refined and enlightened parents, his father being a surgeon, his mother a cultured woman of High Anglican leanings. His parentage meant more for him than is at once apparent. From his father he inherited a scientific inclination and a name of Norse origin. The family's association with Iceland accounts for a certain nordic romanticism and nostalgia which characterises Auden's work. Steeped in the lore of the old sagas and ballads, he was not satisfied until in 1936 he paid a visit to Iceland which resulted in one of his most delightful

8

books, *Letters from Iceland*, published in 1937. His Christian name itself was full of magic, for he was named after Saint Wystan, patron saint of Wistanstow, who, we are told, planted in the ground a stick which grew into a tree. His mother, Constance, who died in 1941, was a native of Somerset and of Norman descent. Her influence on him was profound, as he acknowledges in the *Letters from Iceland*. Perhaps this accounts for his deep religiosity. His friend and collaborator, Christopher Isherwood, tells that at Oxford, "When we collaborate, I have to keep a sharp eye on him, or down flop the characters on their knees (see *F.6, passim*)". And the religious element, as we shall see, far from declining, has been intensified in the gradual evolution of Auden's work.

Another most important factor in Auden's youth was that the family lived in the Midlands. This gave Auden a contact with the realities of Britain's industrial area, and may account to some extent for the quick awakening of his social consciousness in his adolescence. If, as Spender tells us, he abhorred " Nature ", his feelings were deeply stirred by urban and industrial scenes, which indeed provide the characteristic imagery of his poems. In one of his *Letters to Lord Byron*, speaking in praise of the Midlands, he wrote :

> *There on the old historic battlefield,*
>   *The cold ferocity of human wills,*
> *The scars of struggle are as yet unhealed;*
>   *Slattern the tenements on sombre hills,*
>   *And gaunt in valleys the square-windowed mills*
> *That, since the Georgian house, in my conjecture*
> *Remain our finest native architecture.*
> *On economic, health, or moral grounds*
>   *It hasn't got the least excuse to show;*
> *No more than chamber-pots or otter hounds :*
>   *But let me say before it has to go,*
>   *It's the most lovely country that I know;*

Clearer than Scafell Pike, my heart has stamped on
The view from Birmingham to Wolverhampton.
                                    (Letters from Iceland)

And so Auden combined his unusual inheritance in a way which was ultimately to produce a poetry of mysticism and penetrating intelligence, strangely united:

With northern myths my little brain was laden,
  With deeds of Thor and Loki and such scenes;
My favourite tale was Andersen's Ice Maiden;
  But better far than any kings or queens
  I liked to see and know about machines :
And from my sixth until my sixteenth year
I thought myself a mining engineer.
                                    (Letters from Iceland)

The hint about engineering is significant, for as Isherwood has pointed out, Auden's attitude to life and poetry has been scientific, and if Auden has contributed anything positive and particularly challenging to the outlook of his generation of poets, it was through his precept that " I cannot believe that any artist can be good who is not more than a bit of a reporting journalist. " Perhaps this statement finds its equivalent in Rilke's famous *Worker's Letter* of 1921, in which he wrote : " Give us teachers who will praise the Here and Now for us ". For that has been Auden's main occupation.

The poet's education was that of the typical twentieth century bourgeois patrician, save for the exceptional broad-mindedness of his family circle, and that adventurous intellect which soon led him to raise questions of justice, liberty and equality which so many bourgeois are too content to think of asking. He attended private schools, and has given us an entertaining account of his boyhood at Gresham's School, Holt. From this he passed to one of the richest and finest Colleges in Oxford, Christ Church. He was not slow in making

10

his mark in Oxford. He edited collections of Oxford Poetry in 1926 and 1927, on the first occasion with Charles Plumb and on the second with Cecil Day Lewis. His friends, we are told, were few but select; they included many who have since become famous, such as R.H.S.Crossman, Stephen Spender, Rex Warner, Christopher Isherwood. If he had some reputation for eccentricity, keeping a loaded revolver in his desk, banishing, like Wilde, flowers from his room, and working by artificial light during the day, he was reading widely and writing abundantly, as well as obtaining some contact with the realities of politics, if we are to judge from the legends that still circulate in Oxford concerning the hot reception Sir Oswald Mosley was given by young socialists of the University.

Auden's first collection of poems was printed on a hand-press in Oxford by Stephen Spender in 1928, and this volume was substantially reproduced in his first public volume, *Poems,* in 1930. His career after leaving Oxford was disjointed and irregular. He visited Germany in 1929, where he came under the influence, through Layard, of the American psychologist and educationist, Homer Lane. He then taught for various periods in different upper-class private schools. He married Erika, the daughter of Thomas Mann; worked for a few months in films with the G.P.O. Film Unit; drove an ambulance for a short time in the Spanish Civil War, and early in 1939, after a profound disgust with the Munich compromise, he emigrated to America with no intention of returning. In America he taught at Ann Arbor, the University of Michigan; was awarded a Guggenheim research Fellowship; taught for a while at Bennington, and in short displayed the same incapacity for settling down as he had while resident in England. Like many writers his real evolution has been on the intellectual and emotional levels, and the outward phases of his career give little indication of the direction in which he has travelled spiritually.

II

Auden first came into prominence with his *Poems* (1930), published by Faber and Faber. This book, despite its obvious signs of apprenticeship to the poets of the preceding generation, at once set him at the head of the advance guard of poets, and for a decade he set the tone and the fashion to his contemporaries. These poems created some excitement in England, both by their form, which showed an uncommon versatility, and by their originality of subject. The outlook for a young poet in 1930 was not promising. It was a time of economic and social depression. The traditional forms of English verse appeared stale and discredited. T.S. Eliot and Ezra Pound dominated the scene, having combined a great technical achievement in the development of free-verse with an ever narrowing conception of the scope of poetry, setting the fashion for an aristocratic, literary performance heavily bound by tradition; they appeared to be mandarins in the same way as Valéry and Claudel then were in France, and mandarins of the Right. The Sitwells and their followers, who had inherited only the politest relics of Symbolism, such as the fetish of musicalisation, were pursuing an increasing exoticism and preciousness in the manner and substance of their verse. There were really only two poets to whom a young writer could turn for guidance, Robert Graves, who has since accused Auden of plagiarism, and who excelled technically in all forms of verse, but who also was declining into mandarinism, and D.H. Lawrence, who died in that year. Lawrence had, more particularly in his later poems, *Pansies,* developed a vigorous form of free-verse

12

expression which was ideally suited to the creation of a popular poetry, and it soon appeared that in many important respects Lawrence was Auden's immediate master, both in his broad, genial approach to life and letters, and in his free, lively and unconventional use of language. Auden himself has acknowledged this debt, putting Lawrence next to Homer Lane and André Gide :

> Part came from Lane, and part from D. H. Lawrence;
>   Gide, though I didn't know it then, gave part.
> They taught me to express my deep abhorrence
>   If I caught anyone preferring Art
> To Life and Love and being Pure-in-Heart.
> (Letters from Iceland).

To these influences must be added those of Rilke and Kierkegaard, Freud, Jung and Marx. The immediate strong influences of Marx and Freud gave Auden a psychological approach to social evils, and a philosophical conception of the condition of man, which laid the foundation of his later approach to Existentialism. The main role of Auden in his early work was that of Cassandra. As a poetic reporter, his poems survey without pity the disintegration of society and foretell revolution and war, while as a strong under-current is his interest in the neurosis of the individual faced with the impossible task of achieving fulfilment in such a society. All the above elements were already present in Lawrence and nowhere else; but in the place of the strong personal protest of Lawrence, which vitiates so much of his work, Auden had his keen, objective, reporter's sense of scientific observation, based on the firm foundations of Marx and Freud. Nowhere has Auden better expressed the social confusion and depression of the nineteen-thirties than in his first book, and particularly in an early poem written in a metre and style affected by Tennyson in *Maud* and *Locksley Hall*, his two great political poems.

Get there if you can and see the land you once were proud to own
Though the roads have almost vanished and the expresses never run :
Smokeless chimneys, damaged bridges, rotting wharves and choked
    canals,
Tramlines buckled, smashed trucks lying on their side across the rails.
Power-stations locked, deserted, since they drew the boiler fires;
Pylons fallen or subsiding, trailing dead high-tension wires;
Head-gears gaunt on grass-grown pit-banks, seams abandoned years
    ago;
Drop a stone and listen for its splash in flooded dark below.
                              (Poems, XXII).

Auden then continues, putting the blame fairly where it belongs, on the smug and prosperous industrialists of the middle-classes, who failed to adjust themselves to a changing world, thinking the fat days of the Victorian era would last for ever. But the really important aspect of this poem, not from a critical so much as from a social view-point, is that Auden concludes that poetry must be, as Jean-Paul Sartre has since expressed it, *engagée*. The artist, he says, has always been in a minority position :

Lawrence, Blake and Homer Lane, once healers in our English land;
These are dead as iron for ever; these can never hold our hand.
Lawrence was brought down by smut-hounds, Blake went dotty as he
    sang,
Homer Lane was killed in action by the Twickenham Baptist gang.

Auden's words are addressed primarily to the bourgeois intellectuals, and also beyond them to the whole mass of the population :

Shut up talking, charming in the best suits to be had in town,
Lecturing on navigation while the ship is going down.
Drop those priggish ways forever, stop behaving like a stone ;
Throw the bath-chairs right away, and learn to leave ourselves alone.
If we really want to live, we'd better start at once to try;
If we don't, it doesn't matter, but we'd better start to die.

14

So Auden began that " call to action " which gave the impetus to the militant poetry of Spender, Lewis and so many others which was Britain's outstanding contribution in the thirties. Auden also adopted various satirical approaches to his theme. He shows, for instance, how flimsy are the patrician's claims to " leadership ", beneath his confident and assured exterior :

> *Watch any day his nonchalant pauses, see*
> *His dextrous handling of a wrap as he*
> *Steps after into cars, the beggar's envy.*
>
> *" There is a free one ", many say, but err.*
> *He is not that returning conqueror,*
> *Nor ever the poles' circumnavigator.*
>
> *But poised between shocking falls on razor-edge*
> *Has taught himself this balancing subterfuge*
> *Of the accosting profile, the erect carriage....*
>
> *(Poems*, IV).

The picture appears complete, but so far we have only a small impression of what Auden achieved in such poems. It continues :

> *The song, the varied action of the blood*
> *Would drown the warning from the iron wood*
> *Would cancel the inertia of the buried :*
>
> *Travelling by daylight on from house to house*
> *The longest way to the intrinsic peace,*
> *With love's fidelity and with love's weakness.*
>
> *(Poems, IV).*

We are asked to reconcile, in such poems, an acute psychological insight into the decay of a class with a lyric perception of the delights and sorrows of existence, and the transition is accomplished so swiftly, plunging from direct to oblique with so little preparation, that the mundanity of the subject is never allowed to keep the reader long at the level of the commonplace from which the poet starts. It is in such poems as this, despite their remoteness from Lawrence's technique, that we perceive Auden's greatest and enduring gift, a gift he shares with such poets as Lawrence and Blake, that of achieving lyrical expression and maintaining the lyrical flight, however unpromising the material may be. It was through the same capacity for rising from politics into song, indeed transmuting it into song, that Burns became a great national poet, and a poet of the people. Thus Auden's poem develops from a satire of the patrician into a broad human sympathy with that person as a symbol of lost mankind.

The general picture Auden gave of bourgeois society in his first book was depressing, but in itself it was an achievement of first importance to integrate such unpromising material as social criticism into poetry. I know of no other writer on the continent or in America at that time, with the exception of Mayakowsky, who achieved so much. If we recall that this was at a moment when the Surrealists practically dominated France, and when a tide of irrationalism was sweeping over the world, Auden's firm stand for rationality was all the more remarkable. Spender has told us that " Auden arrived at politics by way of psychology ". But already in 1930 he shows a remarkably developed political sense. He was fully conscious of the disintegration of values and the forces which were to produce Hitler and the Spanish War. He painted menacing landscapes, bristling with soldiers and machine-guns; he caught the cries of the guerilla and the whispers of the underground revolutionary. Speaking of Germany in 1929, he wrote :

16

All this time was anxiety at night,
Shooting and barricade in street.
Walking home late I listened to a friend
Talking excitedly of final war
Of proletariat against police —
That one shot girl of nineteen through the knees
They threw that one down concrete stair —
Till I was angry, said I was pleased.

        (Poems, XVI).

Angry at terrorism, pleased at the prospect of revolt, Auden was already groping towards the existentialist problem, becoming conscious that " aloneness is man's real condition " :

Cries in cold air, himself no friend.
In grown man also, may see in face
In his day-thinking and in his night-thinking
Is wareness and is fear of other,
Alone in flesh, himself no friend.

        (Poems, XVI).

So, already according to the existentialist pattern, Auden turns to the insecurity and fear of the individual :

So, insecure, he loves and love
Is insecure, gives less than he expects.
He knows not if it be seed in time to display
Luxuriantly in a wonderful fructification
Or whether it be but a degenerate remnant
Of something immense in the past but now
Surviving only as the infectiousness of disease...

        (Poems, XVI).

From the uncertainty of the individual he passes to the uncertain structure of society :

The falling leaves know it, the children,
At play on the fuming alkali-tip
Or by the flooded football ground, know it —

This is the dragon's day, the devourer's :
Orders are given to the enemy for a time
With underground proliferation of mould,
With constant whisper and the casual question...

(Poems, XVI).

The 'underground proliferation of mould' refers, of course, to the rapid, secret dissemination of both Nazism and Communism, working against each other, multiplying against each other in the dark, preparing on each side for the day of destruction. The climax of the poem comes with a strange admixture of direct Communistic propaganda with the typical key-images of Rilke :

We know it, we know that love
Needs more than the admiring excitement of union,
More than the abrupt self-confident farewell,
The heel on the finishing blade of grass,
The self-confidence of the falling root,
Needs death, death of the grain, our death,
Death of the old gang; would leave them
In sullen valley where is made no friend,
The old gang to be forgotten in the spring,
The hard bitch and the riding-master,
Stiff underground; deep in clear lake
The lolling bridegroom, beautiful, there.

(Poems, XVI).

The poem from which the above extracts have been chosen is central to this book, and gives in its various stages the main outline of Auden's position at that time and reflects also the various methods of composition and statement he affected, varying from the " reporting " of the first extract to the direct, punch-like statement " death of the old gang ", together with a characteristic tension of imagery, in the last, with its added interest of the out-references to Rilke's poetry. The word " adolescent " has sometimes been used as a criticism particularly of these early works; but if it may be applied

18

to the occasional naïve enthusiasm of the arm-chair revolutionary — he who writes " We made all possible preparations, drew up a list of firms " — it cannot in any sense be directed against the maturity of the essential quality of Auden's work, its rich, complex organization. Auden's social criticism is counterbalanced in these poems by a preoccupation with the neurosis of the individual, and on the whole this second group of poems is the more arresting. The individual is baffled, torn between various indecisions, powerless to stem the great destructive forces in society to-day which do so much to nullify the efforts and internal life of the individual :

> *Not even is despair your own, when swiftly*
> *Comes general assault on your ideas of safety :*
> *That sense of famine, central anguish felt*
> *For goodness wasted at peripheral fault.*
>
> *(Poems, III).*

If the " goodness wasted at peripheral fault " means that the qualities of the individual no longer register in the world as a whole, save perhaps — if at all — among one's immediate entourage, the individual also has a peculiar and growing sense of futility against the march of events, and a sense that something familiar and necessary is lost :

> *A bird used to visit this shore :*
> *It isn't going to come any more.*
> *I've come a very long way to prove*
> *No land, no water, and no love.*
>
> *(Poems, IX).*

So the negative note, the same note which describes the social depression, but in this case without the revolutionary exaltation, creeps into the most intimate aspects of existence. Love itself appears sterilised and tainted : Auden's characteristic comments are that love " Designs

his own unhappiness, foretells his own death and is
faithless " (X), or that it " will do murder and betray
for either party equally " (XIV).

It is evident that the defeat-complex of these poems
springs from the author's uncertain allegiance to conflict-
ing ideas. He is, of course, trying to reconcile Freud
and Marx. While he has not become fully aware of the
existentialist position (though he is toying with existentialist problems), he has none of the reassurances that
either a convinced Freudism or a convinced Existentialism could give. The Marxism also is, on the whole,
negative; there is more concern with the sense of
impending disaster than there is with the possibilities
of a powerful collective existence. For the Marxist
there is no question of a strong collective existence still
leaving the individual in the neurotic state depicted
by Auden. Nor can it be said that the neuroses
depicted by Auden are in a spirit of pure reportage,
the necessary corollary to the collapse of the bourgeois
he describes in other poems. The conclusion we must
draw in considering this particular aspect of his work
is that Auden did not fully believe in the curative
properties of Marxism, or did not realise its possible
implications for the individual. Further, maybe he
himself was so involved in the fate of the bourgeoisie
that his pessimism sprang from a realisation that he
could not abdicate from his own doomed social class.
This does not affect our understanding of the impact
these poems made on the generation of 1930, both in
their experimental techniques and their courageous
approach to the social problem of the time.

The " charade ", *Paid on Both Sides*, printed in the
same book, accentuates the general impression of
stalemate between the incapacity for action and the
revolutionary impulse. The main characters are
engaged in some obscure Nordic feud, and all seem

20

constantly aware, even in the midst of violence, of their desire for love and peace. John says :

> *Could I have been some simpleton that lived*
> *Before disaster sent his runners here.*

Trudy speaks even more bluntly :

I am sick of this feud. What do we want to go on killing each other for?
We are all the same.

Seth, the coward, stirs himself into action only by imagining a future of shame and social ostracism, for " Men point in after days ". The only point in quoting from this weakest work of Auden's is as a reminder of the pacifist position implied in Auden's early work, a position which further recommended him at that time to the younger generation.

Auden's next work, *The Orators — An English Study* (1932) gave a rather adolescent and unsuccessful picture of the twentieth-century " hero " in the guise of a young airman. The work, in prose and verse — a form which has its parallels in the work of Raymond Queneau in France and Delmore Schwartz in America — ranges from parody and farce to unsuccessful attempts at high-seriousness. A product of Auden's first school-mastering years, it is not a work on which an adult can linger, though it demonstrates Auden's frequent temptation, working on the theory that the artist should write at all levels, to write occasionally either for the very young or the very stupid. None the less the book has its importance. Here the influence of Homer Lane and Freud have temporarily ousted Marxism, though the Marxist element is present in the young airman's spartan training for his task, as he seeks to de-humanise himself, stripping himself of individuality in order to achieve the delight of perfect function. Perhaps in its way this book was a prophetic picture of the idealism of those who in the Spanish War and in the recent war also attempted such an elimination of self-hood and tried to sublimate their destructive task into an art.

Perhaps Auden's plays, which at this period he began writing with Isherwood, were a more successful attempt at raising the social issues to a mythological plane. By this time Auden, though not a professed Communist, was commonly thought of as such by the young generation. He had already become the symbol of the advance-guard. In 1933 his first dramatic work, a short play in verse and prose, *The Dance of Death*, achieved an instant success and was frequently produced by amateur groups of the working class, particularly of the left, in the provinces. The gist of the play is summed up in the Announcer's opening words : " We present to you this evening a picture of the decline of a class, of how its members dream of a new life, but secretly desire the old, for there is death inside them. We show you that Death as a dancer. " This little play is indeed a brilliant though obvious satire on the " decadence " of the bourgeoisie in the 1930's, and the theme offered opportunity for farce and parody of which Auden took the fullest advantage. Here the communistic element is more strongly marked than in the poems, Karl Marx himself entering in the end, as a *deus ex machina,* to exclaim over the dead dancer " The instruments of production have been too much for him. He is liquidated. " It is small wonder that, for a while, many young Communists thought Auden had rallied completely to their cause.

Auden's subsequent plays have many faults, but they never lost that bright wit, nor that excellent realisation Auden had of the nature of dramatic utterance. With Eliot, Auden did much towards the re-creation of the poetic drama, finding themes of powerful topical interest and seeking a verse medium suitable to their

22

interpretation. *The Dog Beneath the Skin* (1935) was a further step towards complexity with clarity, though still marred by an occasional tendency to the personal " aside " which is one of the weaknesses of his early work.

The theme of this play has all the power of a folk-tale. The heir to the village Squirearchy is lost. Several young men have volunteered, in turn, to set out in search of him, but have never returned. Francis volunteers for the mission and sets out on his quest in the disguise of a dog. The subsequent travels of Francis are, in effect, a dramatisation of that social survey prefigured in Auden's *Poems*. In scenes of broad English humour we are shown a corrupt society in many of its phases, including a brothel scene which is reminiscent of an incident in Joyce's *Ulysses* and a highly surrealist passage in which the hero strips a mannequin. Francis returns to his village, still disguised as a dog, but grown socially more conscious as a result of his travels. Throwing off his disguise he denounces the upper-class hypocrites who are the notabilities of the village, and these worthies show themselves for what they are, suddenly transformed into wild beasts.

The poetry of *The Dog Beneath the Skin* is in the typical, slap-dash style which Auden at that period reserved for his political writings, but the total impression of the play is strong in spite of this and other dramatic weaknesses. It might be described as a " documentary " rather than a play, for there is a narrative line rather than any attempt at genuine dramatic structure. There are no problems of character; the personages in the play are all lay-figures; at times even the narrative line is shaken and we are presented with a series of tableaux. Nor can it be said that Auden had yet succeeded in synthesizing his political and psychological interests; there is no psychological depth, so that the play appears as pure photography, a work without mind.

Much more successful was Auden's next play, *The Ascent of F. 6* (1936). Here the individual is dominant, and Auden's psychology and social satire mingle. We are shown the hero undertaking the ascent of Mount Everest, driven to this gratuitous act (in the Gidean sense) by the ambitions and false values of his parents and bourgeois social milieu, yet inwardly sensitive and fearful. The struggle is that of a man undertaking a task for which he is ill equipped and which he knows will lead him only to failure and death. But in the fulfilment of the Freudian death-wish, the dying hero is beckoned into the arms of the waiting " bride ", his mother. The theme of the sensitive individual lured and destroyed by the false values of a corrupt society is the very heart of Auden's work. We have already noted it in embryo in the " patrician " poem and in *Paid on Both Sides*. It appears later in such satirical poems as the ballad *James Honeyman,* in which the inventor of a new poison gas is destroyed with his family by his own invention, and in the ballad *Victor,* in which an over-innocent young man, nurtured on Boy Scout principles, is driven by his very ignorance of the realities of life to murder his own wife. This form of the *horreur d'être dupe* is a strong element in Auden's psychology and accounts for much of the educative flavour of his work.

If the two plays *The Dog Beneath the Skin* and *The Ascent of F.6* may conveniently be labelled Marxist and Freudian respectively (how strong the influence of Freud was on Auden may be judged from his essay on *Psychology and the Arts* in which he mentioned no other psychologist besides Freud), his best play, *On the Frontier* (1938), is that in which these two major influences are most closely united. Here Auden passed

24

from the concept of the individual versus society to the plane of international catastrophe through a conflict of ideologies. By the device of using a divided stage we are shown a typical family from each of two countries, Westland and Ostnia, living next door to each other with only a wall and a few ideas dividing them. The picture Auden gives of the hypocrisy and veniality of the ruling class, with its obvious satire on the *führer-prinzip*, is subsidiary to the fate of these two families in which is symbolised the destiny of Western civilisation. As the two countries gradually move towards war, the emphasis is shifted from the family unit to the drama of the son and daughter of the two houses who, across the narrow frontier, are in love with each other and constitute the only symbolic bond between two peoples. And they, of course, are doomed to extinction.

This play has, to my mind, lost nothing of its power now that war has come and gone : the theme is still vital and in any case Auden and Isherwood had at last achieved a truly dramatic unity. If the influence of Ernst Toller has to some extent resulted in a symbolic use of character, so that once again depth is lacking, this play represents one of Auden's best attempts in the field of *la littérature engagée*.

III

Meanwhile Auden was developing as a poet, though certain critics still maintained that he had not fulfilled the promise of his first book of poems. Such critics are of two types : those who were opposed to Auden on political grounds, and those, more serious, who like Dr F.R. Leavis, one of our most eminent critics, judged Auden by the highest possible standards and condemned him on the grounds of immaturity and insensibility. The fact remains, however, that by comparison with his immediate contemporaries Auden was not only an innovator of importance, but had a far better grasp of English poetry as a whole and what he could learn from it, as well as a far surer sense of the European situation, than any of them. And the validity of Dr Leavis' criticisms in many respects was not enhanced by his praise of a much inferior poet, Ronald Bottrall, whom Auden has since left well in the rear.

Auden's idiom in his new books was becoming less personal and his technique more sure. With *Look, Stranger!* (1936) and *Another Time* (1940), which should be considered together as representing the period covering the Spanish war and the events leading up to the recent war, Auden largely renounced free verse in favour of more traditional forms.

Look, Stranger! which in America was published under the title *On this Island*, though not Auden's best collection of poems, is rich in its powerful feeling for England, its occasional deep tenderness and its now more matured and well-grounded political conviction. This is Auden's most " social " book, though fundamentally there was no new development in his social approach. He still clung to the recipe of his first poems — " new styles of architecture, a change of heart " — so that the spiritual revolution must precede social reorientation. But now it was expressed with greater lyricism and verbal beauty, as in the magnificent opening of the *Prologue* :

> *O love, the interest itself in thoughtless Heaven,*
> *Make simpler daily the beating of man's heart; within,*
> *There in the ring where name and image meet,*
>
> *Inspire them with such a longing as will make his thought*
> *Alive like patterns a murmuration of starlings*
> *Rising in joy over wolds unwittingly weave;*

Here too on our little reef display your power,
This fortress perched on the edge of the Atlantic scarp,
The mole between all Europe and the exile-crowded sea;

And make us as Newton was, who in his garden watching
The apple falling towards England, became aware
Between himself and her of an eternal tie.

These few lines show perfectly the compelling power of Auden's genuine lyricism and give some idea of his handling of language at its most characteristic. The verse is fluid and harmonious (perhaps conventionally so) and so rich in imagery that it is the image that creates the poem, is the poem. And yet the flight of imagery is here brought down gradually to a point of focus in reality, with the reference to Newton's apple " falling towards England " which in this context is most moving. In his essay on *Criticism in a Mass Society* (Princeton 1941) Auden wrote " The three greatest influences on my own work have been, I think, Dante, Langland and Pope ". Such influences do not, of course, have necessarily any direct expression in a poet's work, nor is there usually any clear correlation to be established once such influences are assimilated. Maybe Dante lurks behind Auden's constant preoccupation with problems of good and evil and sacred and profane love; Pope, behind the reflection of the age and the metrical virtuosity of his poems; Langland, behind the strong sense of social justice and the brilliant sense of England and Englishness which in all Auden's writing is so attractive to the English reader, as the strong feeling of the beauty of France compels us to respect the work of Pierre Emmanuel. This particular poem, the *Prologue,* opens out into that deep feeling for English life and history in a manner almost worthy of Langland :

For now that dream which so long has contented our will,
I mean, of uniting the dead into a splendid empire,
Under whose fertilising flood the Lancashire moss

Sprouted up chimneys, and Glamorgan hid a life
Grim as a tidal rock-pool's in its glove-shaped valleys,
Is already retreating into her maternal shadow;

Leaving the furnaces gasping in the impossible air,
The flotsam at which Dumbarton gapes and hungers;
While upon wind-loved Rowley no hammer shakes

The cluster of mounds like a midget golf-course, graves
Of some who created these intelligible dangerous marvels;
Affectionate people, but crude their sense of glory…

This power of local imagery and reference is a decided advance on Auden's previous work, though the essential message is still unchanged : it is a warning of transformation and disaster, mingled with hope :

Some possible dream, long coiled in the ammonite's slumber
Is uncurling, prepared to lay on our talk and kindness
Its military silence, its surgeon's idea of pain;

And out of the Future into actual History,
As when Merlin, tamer of horses, and his lords to whom
Stonehenge was still a thought, the Pillars passed

And into the undared ocean swung north their prow,
Drives through the night and star-concealing dawn
For the virgin roadsteads of our hearts an unwavering keel.
                                        (Look, Stranger! I).

Auden has also an uncommon felicity in combining, like Donne, the serious and universal with the secondary and particular : his is a poetry of " wit ", and it was this wit which was an important element in gaining for Auden the suffrage of the young intellectuals who, under Eliot's guidance, were familiar with the poetry of the Metaphysicals. As will be seen in a line of the above extracts, this " wit " in Auden's case is sometimes precarious. " The cluster of mounds like a midget golf-course, graves ", is an image of diminution which goes far towards disturbing the balance of the poem. And in the poems of Auden's which fail, the failure is most often due to such lapses of taste as this. But sometimes it is highly successful :

And, gentle, do not care to know,
Where Poland draws her Eastern bow,
What violence is done;
Nor ask what doubtful act allows
Our freedom in this English house,
Our picnics in the sun.

The creepered wall stands up to hide
The gathering multitudes outside
Whose glances hunger worsens;
Concealing from their wretchedness
Our metaphysical distress,
Our kindness to ten persons.

(Look, Stranger! II *).*

Look, Stranger! is full of such bright flashes :

Language of moderation cannot hide;
My sea is empty and the waves are rough :
Gone from the map the shore where childhood played
Tight-fisted as a peasant, eating love...

(Look, Stranger! IX *).*

But perhaps the best poem in the collection is *The Six Beggared Cripples,* a completely successful satirical poem in which a strong irrational element is harnessed to bitter and penetrating social commentary, beginning :

O for doors to be open and an invite with gilded edges
To dine with Lord Lobcock and Count Asthma on the platinum benches,

With the somersaults and fireworks, the roast and the smacking kisses —
Cried the cripples to the silent statue,
The six beggared cripples...

(Look, Stranger ! XXIV).

If this poem is an instance of Auden's capacity for raising
immediate problems to a more universal and symbolic
level — for the " cripples " are all those millions of
socially and psychologically mal-adjusted beings we
call in the twentieth century the " common man ", the
remaining poems are largely developments of those
attitudes already analysed in the 1930 *Poems*. But
meanwhile the Spanish War had broken out, and Auden
at once put his talent at the service of the Left, Republican faction.

Another Time was published in 1940, when Auden
was in America, but it contains his finest and most
important individual poem, *Spain*, first published
in 1937.

Spain is without doubt the central poem in Auden's
work, towards which all his previous efforts at "social-
ising " poetry had been directed. It alone was suffi-
cient to establish Auden as a poet of European stature.
The poem is predominantly lyrical in the highest sense
of the term, though the theme is a political one, handled
largely in psychological terms. The poem opens with
a rapid survey of the past civilisation of Europe :

Yesterday all the past. The language of size
Spreading to China along the trade-routes; the diffusion
Of the counting-frame and the cromlech;
Yesterday the shadow-reckoning in the sunny climates.

Yesterday the assessment of insurance by cards,
The divination of water; yesterday the invention
Of cart-wheels and clocks, the taming of
Horses; yesterday the bustling world of the navigators...

30

> *Yesterday the installation of dynamos and turbines;*
> *The construction of railways in the colonial desert;*
> > *Yesterday the classic lecture*
> *On the origin of Mankind.   But to-day the struggle.*
>
> *Yesterday the belief in the absolute value of Greek;*
> *The fall of the curtain upon the death of a hero;*
> > *Yesterday the prayer to the sunset,*
> *And the adoration of madmen.   But to-day the struggle...*

After building up this tenseness of atmosphere with the repeated " But to-day the struggle ", the poet, the scientist, the people and finally the nations are shown raising their cry of protest and of prayer. They are obviously unwilling to face the situation, expecting some *deus ex machina* to come to their rescue and solve the problem of Spain, as though Spain were only an isolated problem, a single unpleasant event :

> *And the nations combine each cry, invoking the life*
> *That shapes the individual belly and orders*
> > *The private nocturnal terror :*
> *'Did you not found once the city state of the sponge,*
>
> *'Raise the vast military empires of the shark*
> *And the tiger, establish the robin's plucky canton?*
> > *Intervene.   O descend as a dove or*
> *A furious papa or a mild engineer : but descend...'*

And " Life " replies, in the guise of Spain, that life can be whatever the nations choose to make of it, and that what they make of it will depend on what they make of Spain.   There is already more than a hint here of the existentialist conception of time, of the presence of past and future in the single act :

> *'What's your proposal? To build the Just City? I will.*
> *I agree.   Or is it the suicide pact, the romantic*
> > *Death? Very well, I accept, for*
> *I am your choice, your decision : yes, I am Spain.'*

Many have heard it on remote peninsulas,
On sleepy plains, in the aberrant fishermen's islands,
In the corrupt heart of the city;
Have heard and migrated like gulls or the seeds of a flower.

They clung like burrs to the long expresses that lurch
Through the unjust lands, through the night, through the alpine tunnel;
They floated over the oceans;
They walked the passes : they came to present their lives.

On that arid square, that fragment nipped off from hot
Africa, soldered so crudely to inventive Europe,
On that tableland scored by rivers,
Our fever's menacing shapes are precise and alive...

The poem then passes into a consideration of the future, the return to a normality free from terror, only to return relentlessly to the urgent problem of the here and now :

To-day the inevitable increase in the chances of death;
The conscious acceptance of guilt in the fact of murder;
To-day the expending of powers
On the flat ephemeral pamphlet and the boring meeting.

Today the makeshift consolations; the shared cigarette;
The cards in the candle-lit barn and the scraping concert,
The masculine jokes; to-day the
Fumbled and unsatisfactory embrace before hurting.

The stars are dead; the animals will not look :
We are left alone with our day, and the time is short and
History to the defeated
May say Alas but cannot help or pardon.

The composition of this poem is in itself a triumph. It is musically composed and the development might be described as symphonic. The balance of the various aspects of the theme is perfect. The intensity of feeling and high seriousness of the theme and its treatment are well maintained, and in spite of the fact that the poem is built entirely in a series of short, clipped assertions, the rhythm moves smoothly, harmoniously, even with a certain grave nobility. Nor does this poem lose that sense of geniality which is one of Auden's attractive qualities. It is true that objections have been raised to certain passages in the poem which appear to fall from high seriousness and to detract from the tone. One of these is the passage about " A furious papa or a mild engineer ". If this raises a smile it is not a smile that detracts from the poem : it is a tribute, rather, to the witty out-reference to the Freudian explanation of God through the father-complex. Another passage, which has been adversely criticised by the Communist writer Edgell Rickword, is the above reference to " The flat ephemeral pamphlet and the boring meeting ". But it should be understood from the context (quoted above) that Auden was far from deriding such political activities : on the contrary, he was advocating the canalisation of revolutionary feelings into the conventional and necessary though less spectacular channels of party activity. All Auden meant is that sides must be taken, however dreary the upshot of taking sides might appear in practice. In an article on *Auden and Politics (New Verse,* November 1937) Rickword wrote : " Auden has expressed his hatred of Fascism definitely enough, but his failure to analyse the social movement which so profoundly affects his work often leads him to emotionally irresponsible statements. In his poem *Spain* he says :

Today the expending of powers
On the flat ephemeral pamphlet and the boring meeting,

which is an extraordinary example of what used to be accepted as the aloofness proper to the intellectual, in one who has recently been to Spain and had the opportunity of observing the immense vitality which the people are bringing to the task of simultaneously defeating the invaders and creating a free culture.

To-day the struggle, to-morrow the poetry and the fun, that attitude of Auden's would be completely incomprehensible to the Spanish intellectuals to-day. "

The fun to which Rickword alluded is mentioned in the verse :

> To-morrow the rediscovery of romantic love;
> The photographing of ravens; all the fun under
> Liberty's masterful shadow;
> Tomorrow the hour of the pageant-master and the musician...

But Rickword certainly failed to grasp Auden's meaning, for in the general context of the poem the emphasis is upon the struggle of the Spanish war, and the impossibility of a normal life — and a normal life must include " fun " — without the triumph of the Republican cause. Rickword then raised the whole problem of Auden's social position in 1937 : " The lyric grace of Auden's later poems is achieved at the expense of that sensuous consciousness of social change which made his earlier poems such exciting discoveries ". In particular, Rickword thought the handling of social problems in psychological terms was an evasion of the issue, and that there was some danger that Auden might " fall back into the simple exploration of individuality ". It is true that Auden has turned increasingly, since 1936, to the exploration of individuality, but this has not been at the sacrifice of his social interests, though it has perhaps involved the sacrifice of a partisan social attitude. The point is, surely, that an intelligent Communist attitude is not so stiff-necked as that displayed by Mr Rickword in the above comments. Auden had nothing to contribute to the cause but a beautiful and powerful voice, and the discouragement of that contribution on account of a few notes was probably one of the fundamental causes of his gradual separation from orthodox Communism and his increasing scepticism of party politics. While it must be conceded that it is possible to interpret *Spain* as advocating only a temporary allegiance to Communism, as a means of solving the Spanish problem, that does not detract from the poem itself as an admirable statement of the reality of the situation as it was in 1937. For the truth is that the rise of the numbers of Communists in England at that time was not permanent, but represented the only way of expressing a profound sympathy with the workers of Spain in their emergency.

All such commentary should normally lie, so to speak, outside the horizon of a poem, but it cannot do so when a poem is so completely as *Spain* a political statement. It is a great and unique political poem which was not surpassed by any of the " Left " writers in the country at that time. While it was by no means Auden's last " political " poem, it cannot be said that he ever recaptured the lyric enthusiasm and sense of immediacy that it conveyed. Rickword was right, perhaps, in suggesting that the emphasis on the individual can only be achieved at the expense of something else. The abdication to America, which requires no further comment, shows that Auden's life and work developed, in this respect, on similar lines. The English poet writing from America could never hope again to crystallise the thoughts and ideals of his own people in the same way as if he shared their physical existence. The *New Year Letter* of 1941 proves this. But if in Auden a great political and national poet has been lost, perhaps there are other important compensations.

Another Time (1941) is in many ways Auden's best and most representative volume. Though not all the poems are of the high standard of *Spain*, the variety of themes and treatment give a very clear idea of his varied accomplishments as a poet. To measure his achievement we must realise how impossible it would have been for any such volume to have been produced in England ten years previously; for Auden himself had so revolutionised the scope of poetry in that decade that it amounted to a genuine liberation.

The first section *People and Places* might be termed *Poet as Critic,* for it consists mainly of witty, critical poems which go back to Browning in their critical intentions and method. This is a poetry of the intelligence. As a marginal commentary on Kafka there is a poem on *The Law*. There is a brilliant sketch of Edward Lear, " A dirty landscape painter who hated his nose " but to whom " Children swarmed like settlers — he became a land ". Rimbaud, for whom " integrity was not enough " passes by, then Melville, who knew that " No one is ever spared except in dream ". We pause for a moment to consider Pascal's conversion or to see Voltaire at Ferney; there are portraits of *The Composer,* who of all artists is the only one who does not " translate " but who " pours out forgiveness like wine "; or the Novelist, straining after negative capability, who must, like Flaubert, " Suffer dully all the wrongs of man ". In such terms, by a critical approach, Auden was not merely presenting a gallery of his likes and dislikes, but seemed to be reviewing, before America and the war, what remained of Europe, what was the essence of European civilisation and the European mind at its best.

But from such considerations, purely intellectual, the poet passes to an examination of daily life as it has to be suffered, and the picture is dark :

> *O look, look in the mirror,*
> *O look in your distress;*
> *Life remains a blessing*
> *Although you cannot bless.*

> *O stand, stand at the window*
> > *As the tears scald and start;*
> *You shall love your crooked neighbour*
> > *With your crooked heart.*

Miss Gee passes by, a symbol of sterility, a faded spinster who is the victim of false values; the doomed *James Honeyman* works on his poison gases; the innocent *Victor* murders his wife. The *Cabaret Songs* are in the same key:

> *Ten thousand miles deep there in a pit I lay;*
> *But you frowned like thunder and you went away.*

In the *Funeral Blues* there is a typical Audenesque balance between the imagery of the popular song of convention and a genuine tragic feeling:

> *He was my North, my South, my East, and West,*
> *My working week and my Sunday rest,*
> *My noon, my midnight, my talk, my song;*
> *I thought that love would last for ever : I was wrong.*
>
> *The stars are not wanted now : put out every one,*
> *Pack up the moon and dismantle the sun,*
> *Pour away the ocean and sweep up the woods;*
> *For nothing now can ever come to any good.*

As in Auden's very first volume, the social sense is never lost. It penetrates the poignant *Refugee Blues*; it is found even in the most tender and personal love lyrics, including one of his best, that which begins

> *Lay your sleeping head, my love,*
> *Human on my faithless arm...*

and into which which the uncertainties of the outside world fitfully break:

> *Certainty, fidelity*
> *On the stroke of midnight pass*
> *Like vibrations of a bell,*
> *And fashionable madmen raise*

Their pedantic boring cry :
Every farthing of the cost,
All the dreaded cards foretell,
Shall be paid, but from this night
Not a whisper, not a thought,
Not a kiss nor look be lost.

The volume concludes with a heavy sense of loss, in the poem *Spain* and in the Elegies on the death of Yeats, Freud and Toller. In the poem for Yeats, already the clouds of war are gathering, and Auden's outlook is crystallising into a consciousness of universal guilt :

In the nightmare of the dark
All the dogs of Europe bark,
And the living nations wait,
Each sequestered in its hate;

Intellectual disgrace
Stares from every human face,
And the seas of pity lie
Locked and frozen in each eye.

In an article on W.B. Yeats published later in the *Partisan Review*, Auden, in defence of Yeats, claimed that his language was democratic, in the sense of having strength and clarity, and that his poetry was the work and reflection of a " Just man ". The " Just man " was the ideal Auden kept before him during the recent war, and something of the function of this " Just man " is indicated in the closing stanzas of this elegy :

Follow, poet, follow right
To the bottom of the night,
With your unconstraining voice
Still persuade us to rejoice;

> *With the farming of a verse*
> *Make a vineyard of the curse,*
> *Sing of human unsuccess*
> *In a rapture of distress;*
>
> *In the deserts of the heart*
> *Let the healing fountain start,*
> *In the prison of his days*
> *Teach the free man how to praise.*

So by this time Auden had reached Rilke's injunction "Give us teachers who will praise the Here and Now for us", though the task was doubly complex, first because of the war, secondly because of his, by now, full awareness of the existentialist position, the isolation of the individual. The *Dedicatory Poem* (To Chester Kallman) begins :

> *Every eye must weep alone*
> *Till I Will be overthrown.*
>
> *But I Will can be removed,*
> *Not having sense enough*
> *To guard against I Know,*
> *But I Will can be removed.*

In the poem for Ernst Toller there are signs of a mysticism which is grafted uneasily upon Auden's previous social views :

> *We are lived by powers we pretend to understand :*
> *They arrange our loves; it is they who direct at the end*
> *The enemy bullet, the sickness, or even our hand.*

This seeming contradiction is resolved in the brilliant paradox of the poem *September I, 1939*. It was in this poem that his final existentialist position most satisfactorily crystallised, prior to its development in the *New Year Letter* and *The Sea and the Mirror*. Firstly, the isolation of the ego :

39

> *What mad Nijinsky wrote*
> *About Diaghilev*
> *Is true of the normal heart;*
> *For the error bred in the bone*
> *Of each woman and each man*
> *Craves what it cannot have.*
> *Not universal love*
> *But to be loved alone.*

Secondly, both the rejection of external mass authority and rejection of individualism :

> *All I have is a voice*
> *To undo the folded lie,*
> *The romantic lie in the brain*
> *Of the sensual man-in-the-street*
> *And the lie of Authority*
> *Whose buildings grope the sky :*
> *There is no such thing as the State*
> *And no one exists alone;*
> *Hunger allows no choice*
> *To the citizen or the police;*
> *We must love one another or die.*

Here the social and psychological interests of Auden have at last borne fruit, uniting in a strong and positive attitude to life under the influence of Kierkegaard.

IV

Auden's declared attitude to the war was to remain *au-dessus de la mêlée*, but such an attitude proved to be impossible. *New Year Letter* was a desperate and perhaps rather hurried attempt on his part to say his last word on the social and political problems of our time.

It is a commentary on the theme suggested above, that " There is no such thing as the State, and no one exists alone ". The *New Year Letter* is difficult to

40

estimate or to classify. The title itself is so unpretentious as to suggest that, for Auden, it was intended as no more than an interim statement of a point of view or perhaps an attempt to formulate for his own purposes a state of mind of which he himself was uncertain. He chose a rather unsatisfactory verse medium which he handled in such a way as to give an appearance of lightness, enhanced by the close proximity of rhymes, which was by no means appropriate to his message. The heavy accompaniment of notes and out-references suggests that much of his material was not fully assimilated. Allowing for such defects, the poem occupies an important place in Auden's work. It shows, in the first place, what must always be taken for granted in Auden's work, how sensitive Auden was to the whole range of European civilisation, and how direct was his debt to thinkers of all types and views. Tolstoy, Tchekov, Henry James, Kierkegaard, Rilke, Kafka, Köhler, Collingwood, Jung, Groddek — these are only a few of the writers and thinkers whose ideas go into Auden's attempted synthesis. That synthesis is not satisfactory, perhaps, for the reasons mentioned above, but if we are to judge poets by what they attempt, besides what they achieve, it will be noted that Auden was attempting what no poet had tried since Goethe and Wordsworth : to make a synthesis of thought on the condition of man. To those of us who in 1941 expected something more immediate, the poem was disappointing, but after the event it can now be seen that the poet was making an appropriate contribution to his time.

Perhaps the best way of estimating this book would be to indicate some of the problems it raised. The first part of the work opens with certain dogmatisms on the relationship between art and life, a subject which was to be handled more fully later in *The Sea and the Mirror* :

> *To set in order — that's the task*
> *Both Eros and Apollo ask;*
> *For Art and Life agree in this,*
> *That each intends a synthesis...*

But there is the profound difference that art springs from life, isolates aspects of life, and does not control society but reflects it :

> *Art is not life, and cannot be*
> *A midwife to society,*
> *For art is a fait accompli :*
> *What they should do, or how and when*
> *Life-order comes to living men,*
> *It cannot say, for it presents*
> *Already lived experience*
> *Through a convention that creates*
> *Autonomous completed states.*

This statement is, characteristically, supported by long notes and quotations from Hans Spemann's *Embryonic Development and Induction* and Henry James's *Preface* to *The Spoils of Poynton*. Auden also claims that the " Artist, *qua* citizen, is the only person for whom society is really open ", a statement which is best elucidated by reference to Auden's essay *Criticism in a Mass Society* (1941) in which he wrote : " Since the breakdown of patronage in the eighteenth century, the artist has been the extreme case of the free individual, the one for whom, more than for any other, society has become open and untraditional; and in the second place, since art by its nature is a shared, a catholic, activity, he is the first to feel the consequences of a lack of common beliefs, and the first to seek a common basis for human unity ". The above prose quotations show only a part of what is lacking in a characteristic extract from the text of *New Year Letter* itself. In many cases the dogmatic statements on art and life must be subject to such qualification that the poetic text can be taken only as a point of departure since its arguments are so sketchily developed. It is in any case apparent that by 1941 Auden's attitude to art *vis à vis* society was clearly formulated. In the article on Yeats in the *Partisan Review* he even went so far as to say that if there had never been any art or poetry, man's history would not have been materially changed, since art is an end-product and not a shaping force in society. But the paradox is that *New Year Letter* is both a political commentary and an attempt at a revaluation of man. In this respect Auden's precept and example are at variance.

Auden then proceeds, in the poem, to examine the social position of such poets as Dante, Blake, Dryden, Tennyson, Baudelaire and Rilke. As Auden presents them — most inadequately, it must be admitted — they appear somewhat ineffectual, though they stand as symbols of those " who have shown mankind... An order it has yet to find ". With grim humour Auden continues, to show us how " The situation of our time... Surrounds us like a baffling crime ", and we are presented with the body, the suspects, the police. But " the guilt is everywhere ", and in lines of rising passion and indignation the great events of the nineteen-thirties are reviewed and condemned.

In the second part of the poem, Auden approaches the question of individuality, then passes on to examine its relationship to the various mass movements and political ideologies. In examining the problem of good and evil he posits that evil is not the result of free-will, but the illusion of it, and there is only one defence against evil :

> *Against his paralysing smile*
> *And honest realistic style,*
> *Our best protection is that we,*
> *In fact, live in eternity.*

As in 1930, he still dreams of a " change of heart " as the solution to the evils of society :

> *O when will men show common sense*
> *And throw away intelligence,*
> *That kill-joy which discriminates,*
> *Recover what appreciates,*
> *The deep unsnobbish instinct which*
> *Alone can make relation rich,*
> *Upon the Beischlaf of the blood*
> *Establish a real neighbourhood*
> *Where art and industry and mœurs*
> *Are governed by an ordre du cœur?*

Evil is incarnate in the half-truth, the shade of meaning which falsifies, the dualistic view of life, misquotation, vague idealism, false associations. Wordsworth (whose position after the French Revolution was so closely parallel to that of poets of the generation of the Spanish War) is taken as a typical instance of the *homme sensuel moyen* in his reaction against social evolution, duped into rejecting the good with the bad. This second part of the poem, which is by no means the best, ends with the existentialist view that for a man to attempt to live according to a recipe in the form of any ready-made " ideology " is a falsification of his existence. All such solutions as those offered by the great political systems, including Marxism, are shown to be fundamentally hostile to the nature of man.

The third part of the poem is on orthodox Kierke-gaardian lines of Christian Existentialism. There is no sign that Auden has ever been familiar with existentialist philosophy as presented by Sartre and Marcel, and it is unlikely that it would appeal to him, in view of the strong element of Christian morality throughout his own work. He argues, in the familiar terms of Kierkegaard's *Sickness Unto Death* that neither willing nor " willing-not-to-will " can bring man to salvation.

44

We have accidental glimpses of perfect being, but perfect being is not to be achieved or enjoyed; it must be " lost to be regained ", for perfect being itself, on this earth, where all is becoming, cannot endure :

> *Hell is the being of the lie*
> *That we become if we deny*
> *The laws of consciousness and claim*
> *Becoming and Being are the same.*

And this Hell, to Auden's mind, is perfect individualism:

> *Absconding from remembrance, mocked*
> *By our own partial senses, locked*
> *Each in a stale uniqueness, lie*
> *Time-conscious for eternity.*

Heaven, or the perfect society, therefore implies the complete abandonment of Will and the thirst for power over others :

> *We cannot, then, will Heaven where :*
> *Is perfect freedom; our will there*
> *Must lose the will to operate :*
> *But will is free not to negate*
> *Itself in Hell; we're free to will*
> *Ourselves to Purgatory still...*

Thus perfect man, the achievement of perfect Being, is in the freedom — a freedom only attainable in a perfect society or " Heaven " — to renounce will, to abandon the self to a perfectly-ordained universe. Auden has, by a very round-about route, reached the early Christian doctrine of self-abnegation.

Thus it follows that the fall of man came politically — and is constantly repeated — in the desire for power, which is also to be identified with a form of sloth. Looking for a symbol of civilisation, Auden can conceive of none better than England itself, which he celebrates in one of the most moving passages of the poem.

For each of us identifies the crucial realisation of human consciousness in such local symbols as these :

> *In Rookhope I was first aware*
> *Of Self and Not-Self, Death and Dread...*

Speaking again in existentialist terms, Auden states that even if we postulate a complete determinism governing the existence of each individual, there is no evasion of responsibility, it cannot be passed back from the Determined to the Determiner :

> *...Each determined nature must*
> *Regard that nature as a trust*
> *That, being chosen, he must choose,*
> *Determined to become of use.*
> *For we are conscripts to our age,*
> *Simply by being born we wage*
> *The war we are...*

So that, whatever their original determinism, all men are " volunteers " inasmuch as they must choose; no man has the right to master another; in " choosing " no man can choose without reference to all others :

> *Only the 'Idiot' can tell*
> *For which state-office he should run,*
> *Only the Many make the One.*

In a rather too summary account of modern civilisation, covering the tasks which have been undertaken since the Renaissance, the rise and decline of " Empiric Economic Man ", and the critical position of artist and philosopher, among whom

> *Blake shouted insults, Rousseau wept,*
> *Ironic Kierkegaard stared long*
> *And muttered " All are in the wrong "*

46

Auden finally arrives at the position of twentieth-century man :

> *Whichever way we turn we see*
> *Man captured by his liberty,*
> *The measurable taking charge*
> *Of him who measures...*

Science and politics have failed because the common man has not accepted that responsibility which cannot be assumed by the specialist but must be borne by all :

> *Upon each English conscience lie*
> *Two decades of hypocrisy,*
> *And not a German can be proud*
> *Of what his apathy allowed.*

So he returns, in full circle (which gives some measure of the loose and imperfect composition of this poem) to the fundamental problem of Free Will. The conclusion is that " Aloneness is man's real condition ",

> *That each must travel forth alone*
> *In search of the Essential Stone*
> *The 'Nowhere-without-No' that is*
> *The justice of societies.*

Now the real conclusions of Auden's arguments are reached. Firstly, every man is alone and must work out his own human pattern. Secondly,

> *...True Democracy begins*
> *With free confession of our sins;*

a remark which recalls a similar statement of Blake's, or Kafka's comment that we must all pray to each other, and that the writer's work is a prayer. Thirdly, the isolation of man deprives him of the right to power :

> *All are so weak that none dare claim*
> *' I have the right to govern, ' or*
> *' Behold in me the Moral Law '.*

Fourthly, that all individuals belong to one greater unity :

> *And all real unity commences*
> *In consciousness of differences,*
> *That all have wants to satisfy*
> *And each a power to supply.*
> *We need to love all since we are*
> *Each a unique particular*
> *That is no giant, god or dwarf*
> *But one odd human isomorph;*
> *We can love each because we know*
> *All, all of us, that this is so :*
> *Can live because we've lived; the powers*
> *That we create with are not ours.*

The poem concludes with the famous apostrophe beginning " O unicorn among the cedars... to whom no magic charm can lead us ", the only strong lyrical passage in a poem in which lyricism is out of place.

It is evident from the above summary that Auden had nothing to add to the existentialist philosophy on the Christian, Kierkegaardian pattern, but this attempt to give verse expression to it, for all its occasional lameness and disjointedness and solemn levity, may be considered as a step towards some greater work. Jean Wahl has truly said " L'Existence telle que la décrivent les existentialistes risque d'être, en un sens, ce qui existe le moins, une abstraction " *(Existence humaine et transcendance,* 1944). The difficulty of Auden's task was, precisely, that he chose to bring Existentialism down to earth and apply it to contemporary, even topical problems. Some of the main points in his book are well made and firmly established, for instance his reconciliation of the unique particularity of each existence with the conception of unity through co-operation and understanding. The Sartrean philosophy appears, to some, less satisfying in this respect, that it throws the individual back into his own responsibility and despair. In this sense Auden's Existentialism, though it has the Kierkegaardian basis, remains profoundly political, and the general impression of the poem is political rather than religious. If this is the case, it is a caution against describing Auden, in his recent work, as an " Existentialist ", for while the atheistic Existentialism is by him unknown or neglected, the Christian elements of Kierkegaard are not so convincingly integrated as to suggest he has fully accepted them.

V

By contrast with *New Year Letter*, *The Sea and the Mirror* (1945) throws the emphasis upon the individual and individuation, rather than upon the mass of man, the State or the political situation. It is Auden's first attempt at writing a " pure " work that exists in itself (in spite of the dependence on Shakespeare's *The Tempest)* apart from the contemporary scene. And its success is remarkable.

The work of art can only exist by its quality of being arbitrary. Most of the time we are prepared to accept the convention of choice and order by which the artist's illusions are made presentable. But art is not only smaller than existence, it is also infinitely smaller than possible existences. Ultimately it is the artist's own life and capacity for life that determines his principles of selection. If art excludes the possible, yet tries to give the illusion of being, it must always be inadequate to the process of becoming, as is particularly illustrated by the failure of naturalism both in the theatre and in the novel. Such thoughts no doubt occurred to Auden as he reflected critically on the problems raised by Shakespeare's *The Tempest*. What is the metaphysical position of the characters when the play is over, how far have they been true to themselves, what are their potentialities? How just has their creator been towards them? Why not " ask " the characters themselves? What would their opinion be of the situations in which they have been placed then suddenly immobilised for all time? Do they feel grotesquely abandoned? What of the alibis each character has up his sleeve and which the author never allowed him to produce? The villain of the piece assumes a tragic posture as he is dismissed, perhaps secretly hungering for love and understanding; the heroine realises she is trapped into some conventional marriage; the hero begins, now that the heat of action is over, to wonder whether he is really such a fine fellow after all. These are perhaps extra-critical questions, but questions which, though idle in themselves, serve to strengthen critical judgment and help in that difficult task of relating life and art. In *The Sea and the Mirror* Auden has approached such questions at a creative level, much as Browning in his time approached such critical questions in their Renaissance context. It is not at the level of analysis, but at the higher level of poetic criticism, by an orchestration of dramatic monologues which sets the characters themselves into a new relationship with each other. There is a basic ambiguity in the title. It recalls at first the expression that art " holds up the mirror " to Nature, or Arnold's dictum that poetry is " a criticism of life ". In addition, we are led to think of the mirror in the sense of the symbol used in *Alice in Wonderland,* or in Cocteau's *Orphée,* in which it represents the avenue into the life of the imagination and intuition. For Auden, the image is further complicated because on the other side of the mirror — though the mirror may be no more than Art — there exists a more perfect panorama of life as it ought to be than even the ordered universe of Art can show. For him, the mirror of art is two-sided, showing life on the one side, and the eternal life on the other. So the pagan symbol of Lewis Carroll and Cocteau has, for Auden, been sublimated into a magnificent Christian symbol. It is, however, a qualified Christianity, at which he hints in the *Preface* :

> *Which goes to show that the Bard*
> *Was sober when he wrote*
> *That this world of fact we love*
> *Is unsubstantial stuff :*
> *All the rest is silence*
> *On the other side of the wall;*
> *And the silence ripens,*
> *And the ripeness all.*

For on the " other side of the wall " — which in the poem later becomes the equivalent of the " other side of the mirror " — the spirit finds its fulfilment and its complete stature, in the silence of death, or of ever-lasting life.

The characters of *The Tempest* as Auden shows them have nothing in common save the fact that they shared a temporary relationship : each remains funda-mentally isolated in his personality, more or less in the spirit of a line of Auden's earlier poems, " cased in his talent like a uniform ", a line which, incidentally, applies very well to Auden.

The magician, Prospero, whom Shakespeare had left somewhat smug in his consciousness of having done " the right thing ", still remains smug as Auden presents him. But he is already, as he goes about his packing, beginning to have some grave doubts about his past and his relationship to the rest of the world, and particularly his relationship to Ariel, who he feels has grown to dominate him, with Caliban, towards whom he has a feeling of guilt, and towards Antonio, for whom he feels a surprised and sneaking respect.

Perhaps Ariel was not the obedient spirit after all; perhaps Prospero had made the mistake of treating Ariel as a servant, thus intensifying his own imperfection in the wielding of power, or on the other hand, perhaps himself had only been the innocent instrument of Ariel:

> Now, Ariel, I am that I am, your late and lonely master,
>   Who knows now what magic is; — the power to enchant
> That comes from disillusion.   What the books can teach one
>   Is that most desires end up in stinking ponds,
> But we have only to sit still and give no orders,
>   To make you offer us your echo and your mirror...

Prospero, who was shown in Shakespeare's play as a man transmuting life into art, acting as " God " in his " creation " of Caliban, and (mistakenly) confusing life and art the moment he directed his magic to the human end of encompassing his enemy, is now faced with the difficult task of assuming humanity in his abdication of power. The abdication may be an act of will, not of necessity, but it is also an abdication in the face of failure and not, as Shakespeare suggested, at the height of success. Prospero can only assume a tragic role through this sense of defeat. His godliness gradually dissipates in a sense of doubt :

> But Caliban remains my impervious disgrace.
> We did it, Ariel, between us; you found on me a wish
>   For absolute devotion; result — his wreck
> That sprawls in the weeds and will not be repaired :
>
>   My dignity discouraged by a pupil's curse,
> I shall go knowing and incompetent into my grave.

The commentary on Shakespeare is thus at the highest level. Here is the collapse of a noble figure only now become tragic, when the facade of events is removed and the ethics examined. Shakespeare's great play of " reconciliation ", as critics would have it, turns out to have implications of graver import. The existence of a creature deprived of Free Will — this is the crime to be laid at Prospero's door, this is Auden's glimpse of the Inferno, already hinted at in *New Year Letter*. If Caliban has no Free Will, his nature and his sins are directly the responsibility of his creator. Prospero's crime against humanity is that he believed any human dignity could be achieved without free will.

The second chapter follows logically from this revaluation of Prospero's position. If Prospero's sin is in proportion to his outstanding gifts, the remaining characters are re-adjusted accordingly. This chapter is the development of a further existentialist theme, that " aloneness is man's real condition "; that human existences appear discrete and each individual has his own pattern of humanity which he cannot avoid working out. Thus Antonio achieves a certain dignity in the knowledge that he is not intrinsically " inferior " to Prospero : his shortcomings are no doubt on a different scale, but the principle underlying them is the same. Prospero has no monopoly of human wisdom or life. Prospero cannot be so naïf as to imagine he can "abdicate " from his pattern, he cannot deny his artist's temperament and reject magic, for magic will not reject him :

> *Break your wand in half,*
> *The fragments will join; burn your books or lose*
> *Them in the sea, they will soon reappear*
> *Not even damaged.*

Prospero's inability to renounce any part of his humanity, either by assuming or rejecting his role as magician, has no significance in itself, and is significant only in relation to other existences, Antonio says :

> *As long as I choose*
> *To wear my fashion, whatever you wear*
> *Is a magic robe...*

> *As I exist so you shall be denied.*

Antonio sees clearly that Prospero is heading for what Kierkegaard called " The despair of despairing over one's sin ". But it is difficult to tell whether Antonio has really crossed the bridge into self-realisation; as a realist and man of the world he has certainly not yet realised Otherness, he is still the victim of self-hood :

> *Your all is partial, Prospero;*
> *My will is all my own :*
> *Your need to love shall never know*
> *Me : I am I, Antonio,*
> *By choice myself alone.*

Maybe it was Auden's intention, in Antonio, to represent nothing more than the atheistic existentialist.

Antonio's triumphant self-assertion is repeated in various ways by the other characters. Ferdinand has achieved a further step : he is not detained in self-consciousness like Antonio, or even Prospero, but through the love of Miranda has felt the need for an existence of a greater love, a greater existence :

> *I would smile at not other promise than touch, taste, sight,*
> *Were there not, my enough, my exaltation, to bless*
> *As world is offered world, as I hear it tonight*
>
> *Pleading with ours for us, another tenderness*
> *That neither without either could or would possess...*

Stephano is still imprisoned in his flesh, uncertain of spiritual identity or purpose, " a lost thing ", looking for " a lost name ". Gonzalo is an image of defeat, convicted, like Prospero, of " Doubt and insufficient love ". Alonso, like Prospero, has now realised the futility of power, for he, like Ferdinand, has heard a higher voice, has realised the potentialities of love :

> *Having heard the solemn*
> *Music strike and seen the statue move.*

The " villain ", Sebastian, unsuccessful and discredited, realises that there was a flaw of charity in his viciousness; he had thus failed to be the self he had willed, but he still remains the unhappy victim of the will to power. Miranda, singing her exquisite, metaphysical song " My dear One is mine as mirrors are lonely " has, through love, bridged the gulf between rational and irrational, living in that enchanted state between the two, privileged, like a child — or as perhaps Prospero once was — to exist simultaneously in the realms of truth and dream.

We are tempted to regard the long speech of Caliban to the Audience as the most important part of *The Sea and the Mirror,* because it elucidates so many difficult points; but it should not be considered apart from the foregoing speeches, all of which emphasise the importance of plural existences, while they comment on the misrepresentation of the author in *The Tempest.* Caliban represents Demos awakening to consciousness, man questioning his masters and his maker. The indictment of all concerned, the passive crowd, the biassed and fuddled creator, the artist's imperfect vision, the arbitrary Muse, is one of the finest passages in Auden's work. Caliban first speaks on behalf of the audience, and the main point of his inquiry is to show that Caliban, (who is here speaking " out of turn " by answering the questions himself) was not an art-conception, and that either the Author introduced Caliban by way of revenge on the Muse (Shakespeare's last word) or else he did so out of sheer ineptitude. Shakespeare showed, in Caliban, the " exception " who has no place in the ordered world of art. If Art and Life must remain separate — for the living man cannot breathe in the atmosphere of art, any more than Ariel could bear to be a civil servant — then it was a mistake to represent Caliban at all and thus introduce the real into the element of the symbol. While all existences make "one public whole" in which "We and They" are united, this "whole" cannot be represented in Art, so that realism in art is undesirable and in fact impossible. Caliban says to the author : "You yourself, we seem to remember, have spoken of the conjured spectacle as 'a mirror held up to nature', a phrase misleading in its aphoristic sweep but indicative at least of one aspect of the relation between the real and the imagined, their mutual reversal of value, for isn't the essential artistic strangeness to which your citation of the sinisterly biassed image would point just this : that on the far side of the mirror the general will to compose, to form at all costs a felicitous pattern, becomes the necessary cause of any particular effort to live or act or triumph or vary, instead of being as, in so far as it emerges at all, it is on this side, their accidental effect ? "

Both art and nature are incomplete, though creating each other, and their essential difference lies in the one's love of order creating a pattern of life, whereas the other tends unconsciously to a massive pattern merely as a result of numerous existences being lived. The co-presence of Ariel, the "spirit of reflection" and of Caliban, the gross human substance of life, in one play, is in effect a heresy, the violation of both art, where Caliban does not conform to pattern, and life, where Ariel is an affront to an organic society. Since Art is in itself finite, the "magic" of their co-presence is a falsification, since "magic" pre-supposes the infinite. Could Caliban have been presented in any other way? Not in so far as he is a creature, "His distorted parody, a deformed and savage slave ", yet a slave in the image of his Creator. Caliban even hints that the presentation of Ariel might be similarly in bad taste, an insult to the real : "For if the intrusion of the real has disconcerted

56

and incommoded the poetic, that is a mere baga-
telle, compared to the damage which the poetic would
inflict if it ever succeeded in intruding upon the real ".
The infliction of the perfection of art upon life is death.

Caliban now changes his role and speaks for the
author. He shows how precarious is the artist's reliance
upon Ariel or imagination, for at some stage Ariel is
likely to assume the role of Caliban. This is because
the disciplines of Art reduce the sphere of Free Will,
and the result is horror.

Finally, Caliban speaks on behalf of Ariel and himself.
There is nothing intrinsically new in the brilliant pages
which follow (47-55) which are a concrete exposition
of Kierkegaard's *Sickness unto Death*. The alternative
choices are shown of the " Despair of willing to be
oneself" and the " Despair of not willing to be oneself".
But if it is easy to disengage such alternatives, how can
the artist possibly hope to achieve a genuine synthesis
comparable to that of real existence? Naturalism
obscures essential truth by excess of detail, yet to aim
at this truth is the artist's task : " and ultimately, what
other aim and justification has he, what else exactly is
the artistic gift which he is forbidden to hide, if not
to make you unforgettably conscious of the ungar-
nished offended gap between what you so unquestio-
nably are and what you are commanded without
any question to become, of the unqualified NO that
opposes your every step in any direction ? " It appears
Caliban is something of a determinist. And the failure of
the artist merely reflects man's inability to live life as it
might be lived, while in its usual state life reminds one
of " the greatest grand opera rendered by a very provin-
cial touring company indeed ".

The conclusion of the work is, like that of the
New Year Letter and the sonnet-sequence *The Quest*
(a quest for the right mode of existence) both existentialist

and Christian. Now we are shown the possibilities behind the mirror, beyond art, towards which art so inadequately strives. The " better life " is behind and beyond art. The actors themselves are occasionally aware of a better possible script as they repeat the poet's words. And that better script is " The Word which is our only *raison d'être* ". The stage itself, they realise, is only a poor, tattered symbol of " That wholly Other Life from which we are separated, by an essential emphatic gulf of which our contrived fissures of mirror and proscenium arch — we understand them at last — are feeble prefigurative signs ". Art as we achieve it can only be symbolic of a greater and higher art : " It is just here, among the ruins and the bones, that we may rejoice in the perfected Work that is not ours ". And, fittingly, the book ends with the reconciliation of Ariel and Caliban.

From this Christian conclusion, there is a logical transition to a wholly Christian work, Auden's Christmas Oratorio : *For the Time Being*. We do not need to analyse this work in detail since the same principles obtain as in *The Sea and the Mirror*. It is perhaps characteristic of Auden — and this is one of the reasons why critics often distrust him — that the process of working towards a Christian way of life was much more attractive than its achievement. For this reason the Oratorio lacks the fire and conviction of *The Sea and the Mirror*. The nativity theme is a convenient objective-correlative into which Auden's view of the world situation is translated. The miracle of the Nativity is but a response to a need, a gesture of improbable justice to an unhappy world. Symbolically the faculties of man are shown disunited, longing for unity. The central point is that the price of the miracle of Christ's birth was the suspension, in one person (Mary) of Free Will, for Gabriel answers Mary :

Since Adam, being free to choose,
Chose to imagine he was free
To choose his own necessity,
Lost in his freedom, Man pursues
The shadow of his images :
Today the Unknown seeks the known ;
What I am willed to ask, your own
Will has no answer ; child, it lies
Within your power of choosing to
Conceive the Child who chooses you.

So the beauty of the miracle lies in the surrender of Mary's Free Will to God's will, and it is a glad surrender. Beside this perfect recognition of the essence of the theme, the remainder of the work appears to be at a less exalted level. There are only two other passages of real power : the Meditation of Simeon and the Massacre of the Innocents. The Meditation is on orthodox and unoriginal lines. Herod's monologue in The Massacre of the Innocents recalls Eliot's presentation of the Barons at the end of *Murder in the Cathedral*. As an essay in the genre of Caliban's speech it is excellent and highly amusing, but the tone of Herod's speech, though in character, has the unfortunate result of falsifying the tone of the Oratorio as a whole. Auden has not yet learnt to hold his humour in check at the right moment.

VI

Auden's most recent book *The Age of Anxiety* is in many respects disappointing as a literary production, but it shows a further development in the direction of Existentialism, and enables us to complete our picture of Auden's activity during the war period. The book is described as a " baroque eclogue ", though it is baroque only in the sense of being rough in form and wayward in fancy : if it can at all be regarded as an " eclogue ', it is only in the extended sense given to that word by Empson in *Some Versions of Pastoral*. The work has no true dramatic quality, and only a thin, prose narrative line unites a series of monologues uttered by four rather unoriginal characters sitting in a bar in New York, some time during the War. These four people, each imprisoned in his own *so sein*, strive for a brief period to achieve a group-existence by pooling their outlook and temporarily escaping from themselves and the outside world. At the end they disperse, fundamentally unchanged yet no doubt spiritually enriched by their experience. There is probably some symbolic value in the fact that the love-situation achieved by Rosetta and Emble does not result in consummation.

The characters are disillusioned intellectuals of the type commonly portrayed by Auden and Isherwood in their plays : and this type rather belies the author's attempt to differentiate between them by drawing them from different walks of life. Quant, an Americanised Irishman, tends to read Mythology when he is out of work, and for the rough diamond he is supposed to be he has a surprising knowledge of classical literature. Malin is a " Medical Intelligence Officer " on leave, a man with a scientific background, in fact a University lecturer, who is given to making sad and profound comments about " Life ". Emble, who is in the Navy after attending some Mid-West University, is a not very interesting young man whose main attraction is a certain callowness. Rosetta, the central figure of the eclogue, is a beautifully drawn character symbolising that nostalgia which is the centre of Auden's work. She is better than her background suggests, a rather conventional background of a displaced Englishwoman working as a buyer for a departmental store, and who has odd memories of a " county " childhood of hunts, balls and parties which seem a little out of focus and out of date.

It is our belief that it is because Auden has not a full grasp of Existentialism, and for no other reason, that he has given his creations so many of the attributes that are the mainsprings of his early work : he has not yet put aside his heavy reliance on Freud, Groddeck and his earlier gods. All four characters appear to have strong pacifist leanings : Rosetta has a powerful father-fixation, while Quant, Emble and Malin have a pervading sense of guilt which is associated with thoughts of their mothers (pp. 62, 83, 85, 124). Quant and Malin are haunted by a sense of failure which they sometimes discuss in terms of " success " (pp. 14, 47). Malin and Emble are victims of anguish (pp. 13, 21, 86, 125), while Quant suffers from an inexplicable nausea (pp. 34, 38, 42, 84, 86) and Rosetta is afraid of freedom (p. 71). They deal with the subject of time in a way which shows that their creator has not yet read *L'Être et le Néant* (but he will). Whereas Sartre holds that we are only what we are now, at this given moment, Rosetta is " sick of Time " (p. 92) and does her best to reject it altogether. Quant represents modern man as being a slave to time (p. 44) yet speaks of the " continuous Now " (p. 45). One's general impression is that what existentialist elements there are in the outlook of the characters are not easily reconcilable to the time outlook of Dunne and Eliot, or to the psychologies of Freud and Jung, which also appear in the eclogue.

It is not our intention to analyse the work from the point of view of its thought or philosophy, for the important question which arises is whether Auden is developing as a poet. It is claimed for this book that " the form is one more illustration of the author's inexhaustible mastery of versification, which becomes more astonishing with every work he puts forth ". With this we entirely agree : on the technical side this book confirms what even Auden's most violent critics have never denied, that he has great skill as a craftsman. The word " form ", however, suggests something more important than mere versification, and here we must go beyond the terms of the title " baroque eclogue " to consider its semi-dramatic nature.

The main weakness of the work is not technical, but lies in its faults of tone, which could easily be rectified, and more seriously in a certain failure to use language dramatically, a failure to adapt language to its various mouthpieces. Almost any of the speeches with the exception of Rosetta's might have been spoken by any of the characters. There is little attempt to select language in such a way as to ensure any psychological differentiation.

The general tone of the work is belied by the first sentence of the Prologue : "When the historical process breaks down and armies organize with their embossed debates the ensuing void which they can never consecrate, when necessity is associated with horror and freedom with boredom, then it looks good to the bar business ". Either the ' historical process ' is accepted as a nineteenth-century political concept as something which does not break down, or it is dismissed as a meaningless phrase : but Auden values the ' historical process ' and his irony misses fire. The unpleasant breeziness of the final words ' good for the bar business' is reinforced by the association ' freedom-boredom '. The rather bluff opening of the work is weak, and is very soon belied by the youthful seriousness of the protagonists. We draw attention to this, not because we consider the tone of the work as a whole to be imperfect, but because critics have not been slow to pounce on such lapses as " perambulate our paths and pickles " and " God's in his greenhouse, his geese in the world ". Some of the juke-box songs in the book might allow such language, but on that level also the poet is uncertain : for instance Quant's song "Let me sing you a song, the most side-splitting tale " is a complete failure. We have already remarked on Auden's tendency towards faults of tone, and it is not likely that prolonged residence in America will bring improvement. Such writers as Henry James and Eliot, adopting the English way of life, gained immeasurably by developing in an atmosphere in which they felt their solidarity with English writers in a place and time where English could best be written. Auden is obtaining in America a broad and enriched view of existence, as *The Age of Anxiety* shows, but at the cost of a certain spiritual isolation and the loss of certain critical standards.

Though throughout the work we remain conscious of the purely intellectual position of Malin, the direct, matter-of-fact tone of Quant, the youthful idealism of Emble, they only come to life towards the end of the book, and on the whole their speeches are not frequently characteristic. For instance, there is nothing to choose between these statements of Malin and Quant :

> Malin : *He pines for some*
> *Nameless Eden where he never was*
> *But where in his wishes once again*
> *Over hallowed acres, without a stitch*
> *Of achievement on, the children play*
> *Nor care how comely they couldn't be*
> *Since they needn't know they're not happy.*

> Quant : *So do the ignored.   In the soft-footed*
> *Hours of darkness when elevators*
> *Raise blondes aloft to bachelor suites*
> *And the night-nurse notices a change*
> *In the patient's breathing, and Pride lies*
> *Awake in himself too weak to stir*
> *As Shame and Regret shove into his their*
> *Inflamed faces, we failures inquire*
> *For the treasure also.*

In this book Auden has made very free use of alliterative devices, and with obvious success. The work
gathers impetus gradually until by the third part,
The Seven Stages, we come to some really fine writing.
But it is a mistake in construction to vary the style and
technique from section to section of the work, rather
than from character to character. If we consider as an
example one of Quant's speeches, we notice also that
there is an impressionistic technique which results in
some strange shifts of emphasis and variations of tone :

> *Orpheus lies*
> *Violently slain on the virid bank,*
> *That smooth sward where he sinned against kind,*
> *And, wild by the water, women stone*
> *The broken torso but the bloody head*
> *In the far distance floating away*
> *Down the steady stream, still opening*
> *Its charming mouth, goes chanting on in*
> *Fortissimo tones, a tenor lyre*
> *Dinning the doom into a deaf Nature*
> *Of her loose chaos. For Long-Ago has been*
> *Ever-After since Ur-Papa gave*
> *The Primal Yawn that expressed all things*
> *(In His boredom their beings) and brought forth*
> *The wit of this world. One-Eye's mistake*
> *Is sorry He spoke.*

The skill with which the alliterative system is control-
led is beyond dispute. And though we are surprised to
find the Orpheus theme thus handled by the hard-boiled
Quant (who elsewhere treats us to a rather inferior
parody of Baudelaire's *Le Voyage à Cythère*), there is no
doubt that it is well done, in spite of certain conventional weaknesses (*far, away, steady, charming,* etc.) The
final statement, however, comes as a rather unpleasant
fall into pretentious parody. Quant merges too frequently into the terrain of Malin and Emble, and often
speaks in turn rather than in character.

64

Rosetta, with her marked " Room of One's Own " outlook, is the only satisfactorily developed personage, the only one who really achieves a *literary* significance. This is perhaps because she is a creature of imagination, somewhat idealised, and not limited by the conventional realism which destroys the menfolk. All the most brilliant writing of the book goes into her speeches. Though she gives a rather nineteen-fourteenish picture of England (p. 21) and though her version of the " Fourth Age " of man seems out of place (p. 41), she is successfully portrayed as intelligent and intuitive. sensitive to all that escapes the others : she is a poet and a dreamer. Her song " Deep in my dark the dream shines " is the finest lyric in the book. It is in reading Rosetta's lines that we are most forcibly reminded that *The Age of Anxiety* must be thought of primarily in terms of speech, and not just as a written literary production. Though it is not strictly dramatic, it demands performance, and the type of performance for which it is best suited is obviously the radio. Auden, we begin to think, is still destined to develop the line which Lawrence and Eliot had in common, the line of common speech which sought to develop the vocabulary of poetry in breadth as well as intensity. Perhaps for this reason he does not sustain the purple passage but returns nervously to earth. Space forbids more than a rapid glance at a typical speech from Rosetta :

> *Yet holy are the dolls*
> *Who, junior for ever, just begin*
> *Their open lives in absolute space,*
> *Are simply themselves, deceiving none,*
> *Their clothes creatures, so clearly expressing,*
> *Tearless, timeless, the paternal world*
> *Of pillars and parks. O Primal Age*
> *When we danced deisal, ou dream-wishes*
> *Vert and volant, unvetoed our song.*
> *For crows brought cups of cold water to*

Ewes that were with young; unicorn herds
Galumphed through lilies; little mice played
With great cock-a-hoop cats; courteous griffins
Waltzed with wyverns, and the wild horses
Drew nigh their neighbours and neighed with joy,
All feasting with friends.   What faded you
To this drab dusk?   O the drains are clogged,
Rain-rusted, the roofs of the privies
Have fallen in, the flag is covered
With stale stains, the stable-clock face
Mottled with moss.   Mocking blows the wind
Into my mouth.   O but they've left me.
I wronged.   Then they ran.   I'm running down.
Wafna.   Wafna.   Who's to wind me now
In this lost land?

Though there is considerable latitude here in the use of colloquial speech (the second phrase being reminiscent of common schoolgirlish jargon) there is a fine poise about this writing. Beginning with the Rilkean evocation of the dolls as symbols of childish perfection and innocence, there is a logical transition to the evocation of a golden age which is also the fabulous golden age of childhood. But towards the end the familiar symbols broaden, until the " I " is not merely the girl Rosetta, but civilisation itself. We can judge from the ease with which Auden obtains his effects and handles his medium, that his essential gifts as a poet are still undimmed, though rarely so concentrated as here. We note once more however that the best passages in the book (and usually in Auden's work as a whole) are nostalgic, but that in this case the nostalgia is magnificently subordinated to the sense of evil which is so swiftly and logically introduced (" I wronged ") as to give a sudden and complete explanation of the fading of the earthly paradise.

The *Epilogue*, and particularly the concluding speech of Malin, indicates that the promise held out by *The*

Sea and the Mirror may yet be realised. Some readers may find a significant lack of true religious background, though not of religious feeling, in the work, and may find the introduction of God into Malin's last speech both unexpected and misplaced. Though the speech has the usual faults of tone (the half-hearted colloquial jests in nature's " lost lollypop " and our bodies' " childish Ows ") it contains at least one passage of firm and mature writing :

> *We belong to our kind,*
> *Are judged as we judge, for all gestures of time*
> *And all species of space respond in our own*
> *Contradictory dialect, the double talk*
> *Of ambiguous bodies, born like us to that*
> *Natural neighbourhood which denial itself*
> *Like a friend confirms; they reflect our status,*
> *Temporals pleading for eternal life with*
> *The infinite impetus of anxious spirits,*
> *Finite in fact yet refusing to be real,*
> *Wanting our own way, unwilling to say Yes*
> *To the Self-So which is the same at all times,*
> *That Always-Opposite which is the whole subject*
> *Of our not-knowing, yet from no necessity*
> *Condescended to exist and to suffer death*
> *And, scorned on a scaffold, ensconced in His life*
> *The human household.   In our anguish we struggle*
> *To elude Him, to lie to Him, yet His love observes*
> *His appalling promise...*

It matters little to us whether the poet's beliefs are well-founded, though it is certain that without beliefs he cannot be a poet. We have seen what Yeats could do, starting from what appeared to be a hollow esoteric mysticism, or Eliot from the borrowed ritual of an heretical church. Auden's capacity for development does not depend on the truth or untruth of Existentialism, but on the inspiration it can give to him as a poet. To the existentialist values of self, time, anguish and the like he freely adds the symbols of psychology and religion, while such an extension would be impossible for anyone starting from the other end. *The Age of Anxiety* is a rough and unsatisfactory work, like all those Auden has produced since 1940, precisely because he is advancing into new territory in a way which demands not only an enlargement of his knowledge, but the invention of new forms of expression. Although Auden is now in his forties, the peculiar direction of his development suggests that his powers have not yet crystallised because he has chosen a difficult path, and we reject the thesis that those powers have not matured since 1930. Landmarks in his work since that time have been *Spain*, the sonnets in *A Journey to a War*, the *Elegy on the Death of Yeats*, several passages in the *New Year Letter*, and *The Sea and the Mirror*. The success of *The Age of Anxiety* is only partial : it is a technical success, rather than a success in form. The eclogue as such does not favour marked variations of character, and as Auden handles it we are sometimes aware of a striving towards dramatic unity which is perhaps misplaced. It is none the less a most interesting production and one which again demonstrates an unquestionable originality of mind.

It is not the purpose of this study to attempt any assessment of Auden's position as a poet, nor to prophesy about his future. To do him justice we must bear in mind the many defects of his work. If it has evolved satisfactorily, on the whole, from the early emphasis on Freud and Marx to a more universal level on the side of content, and if his diction has progressed from an ingenuous privacy to a clear and democratic speech, there are certain reservations to be made. Freud, Marx, Kierkegaard — these certainly show Auden to be a " conscript to his age " and certain critics might justifiably detect a will-to-be-fashionable.

Those, however, who are always longing to know " where Auden stands ", miss the drama of his work, which is precisely its restless evolution, its refusal to adhere to a formula. His marxism never convinced Marxists; his psychology was always incomplete and wayward; his Existentialism is only partial, and still tinged with reminiscences of Marx and Freud. His Christianity is still too tinged with satire to amount to meek acceptance. What is interesting, however, is the gathering synthesis of all these elements.

Perhaps we have paid too little attention in this study to Auden's craftsmanship as a poet, but the various extracts give some indication of his manner. Auden has not been a great innovator so much as a great reviver; he has done more than anyone in the past fifteen years to remind us of the wealth of metres and rhythms at our disposal in English. His greatest fault is his uncertainty of tone; he tends too often to treat really serious matters in tones of jest and banality, while occasionally giving pompous utterance to platitudes. He tends to credit his readers with no background of knowledge, and many things are " explained " — for instance in the *New Year Letter* — which had better been implied. It is this fault which most justifies the accusation of immaturity. The fact that Auden is the most adventurous and provocative, and occasionally the most sensitive and most skilled young poet writing in English today, sets our contemporary poetry in its perspective.